Bipp Treatment of War Wounds

BIPP TREATMENT OF
WAR WOUNDS

PUBLISHED BY THE JOINT COMMITTEE OF
HENRY FROWDE AND HODDER & STOUGHTON
AT THE OXFORD PRESS WAREHOUSE
FALCON SQUARE, LONDON, E.C. 1.

BIPP TREATMENT
OF WAR WOUNDS

BY

RUTHERFORD MORISON

PROFESSOR OF SURGERY, DURHAM UNIVERSITY ;
SENIOR SURGEON, NORTHUMBERLAND WAR HOSPITAL

LONDON

HENRY FROWDE   HODDER & STOUGHTON

OXFORD UNIVERSITY PRESS   20, WARWICK SQUARE, E.C.4

1918

PRINTED IN GREAT BRITAIN BY
RICHARD CLAY AND SONS, LIMITED,
BRUNSWICK STREET, STAMFORD STREET, S.E. 1,
AND BUNGAY, SUFFOLK.

PREFACE

WAR has taught surgeons once more the value of Lord Lister's work on the use of antiseptics in Wound Treatment, and now it has been proved that with their aid primary union after suture of infected, suppurating wounds is possible. A long surgical experience may be of the greatest value, but in my case it was a handicap, for it took me a long time to realise the truth of what I saw —so opposed was it to all ordinary surgical canons. This small book has been written by request as a War contribution, and in it I have endeavoured to avoid two difficulties which I feared. The first concerned an explanation of our results which I knew would plunge me into ventures from which I could not escape unscathed ; the second was to avoid any over-estimation, from excess of enthusiasm, of the value of this method of wound treatment.

The best manner of accomplishing these ends seemed to be by limiting the information offered to what I knew, and by rejecting any other matter, however interesting it might be.

The book is an account of our method of Wound Treatment, and it is so simple that a *clever* surgeon is unnecessary for the achievement of the best results, though a *careful* one is essential.

March, 1918.   R. M.

BIPP TREATMENT OF WAR WOUNDS

WOUND treatment during the last twenty years had reached such perfection that surgeons had almost concluded that they were masters of the situation when the War came and awakened them to reality.

Many then expressed the view that War wounds were as bad as those of fifty years before, but that was because few had actual experience of so long ago. The War wounds were bad enough—painful, incapacitating, healing slowly and with large indurated scars, but, however ill they made their victim, seldom deadly ; those of fifty years ago, especially when involving bones, terminated as often in death from septic infection as in recovery—a difference of vital importance. The explanation is simple. Our War wounds, after treatment was instituted, were spared further infection from outside ; the wounds of fifty years ago were infected anew after every surgical manipulation. We wash our hands *before* operations, the older surgeons washed theirs *after* the operation was over.

The first year of the War was one of unhappy surgical experience. Though the mortality in home hospitals was very small, everyone soon learned that free drainage and frequent dressings were the only safe measures, and that beyond these the less done to the wounded the better they recovered. Any opening up of fresh surfaces was likely to be followed by local and general signs of inflammation, such as increased suppuration and fever, and the most unpromising looking conditions were often left alone because of the fear of a " septic flare-up " after any surgical interference.

Towards the end of the year 1915, disheartened by the results of this treatment, I gradually developed a new method of dealing with infected wounds, which has been proved efficient. Though not yet ideal in results, it is more nearly so than any other so far evolved.

My conclusion now is : *That if it is possible to get to the bottom of an infected wound so that it can be thoroughly cleansed mechanically, and suitable antiseptics be applied, the wound can be closed at once with interrupted sutures, always with impunity, and many times with the prospect of finding it healed when the dressing is removed for the first time at the end of three weeks.* This fact has been proved by hundreds of cases and establishes a new Principle in Surgery, though details of the method can doubtless be improved. For example, in our early cases pure carbolic acid was used as an important adjunct. We have now with advantage omitted this.

Because these patients are already handicapped by infective organisms it is the more

9

essential that all the precautions at present taken by careful surgeons for ordinary wounds should be used for them. The strictest surgical cleanliness in operating theatres and surroundings should enter into the scheme of treatment, and all who take part in it should wear smooth indiarubber gloves which can be cleansed by washing in antiseptics, sterile garments, masks and caps.

Summary of Technique

1. Under an anæsthetic, usually upon ether, cover the wound with gauze wrung out of one in twenty carbolic acid, and clean the skin and the surrounding area with the same lotion.

2. Open the wound freely and, if possible, sufficiently to permit of inspection of its cavity. A guide—a finger is the best if the size of the wound permits of it, and if not a thick probe—should be introduced to the bottom of the wound and held there and

10

fully exposed. In doing this special regard must be paid to nerve-trunks and muscular branches of nerves, since the division of blood-vessels, excepting the largest, and of muscles themselves does little harm as compared with that of the disability following nerve damage. Cleanse the cavity with dry sterile gauze mops, Volkmann's spoon, etc., and remove all foreign bodies.

3. Mop the surrounding skin and the wound cavity with methylated spirit and dry it.

Put Bipp in the wound,* rub it well in with dry gauze, then remove all excess,

---

* Preparation of the paste :—Iodoform, 16 oz. ; bismuth subnitrate, 8 oz. ; liquid paraffin, 8 fl. oz., or a sufficient quantity. The powders are mixed together in a clean mortar, and the liquid paraffin incorporated. The quantity of liquid paraffin required varies according to the bulk of the powders, the bismuth in particular being liable to a considerable variation in bulk. A sufficient quantity should be added to form a thick paste. It is then advisable to rub down the paste in small quantities at a time, on a slab with a spatula, to ensure freedom from grit and other particles of powder. This paste is not specially sterilised.

11

leaving only a thin covering over the wound surface. Dress the wound with sterile gauze and cover all with an absorbent pad, which is to be held in position by sticking plaster and a bandage. This dressing requires no change for days or weeks if the patient is free from pain and constitutional disturbance. Should, however, discharge come through, the stained part must be soaked in spirit and a gauze dressing wrung out of the same applied as a further covering, or a fresh dressing should be made.

Redressing is very simply done. After removal of the old dressings the wound is covered with a dossil of wool soaked in spirit, and any sticky, dirty-looking discharge is wiped off the surrounding skin until it is clean.

Though it is desirable to see the bottom of *all* wounds, it may be occasionally unwise. A through-and-through wound, with small entrance and exit openings, may be *generally* cleansed satisfactorily by passing a long strip of gauze through it and pulling this to and fro as a first step, next by doing the same with a strip of spirit gauze, and finally depositing a layer of Bipp on the inner surface of the wound by spreading a long strip of gauze with the paste, passing it through the track and rubbing in the medicament by pulling the gauze backwards and forwards again and again.

Dissecting out the wound is unnecessary, and in the hands of surgeons who are insufficient anatomists may be dangerous. The most that should be done in this respect is to remove only such portions of tissues as are obviously dead. The drier a wound can be made the better, but some hæmorrhagic oozing does not bar success.

When the first dressing has been removed, if the wound is clean, granulating and superficial, healing may be hastened by a change to ordinary treatment.

Though we have bacteriological proof that the discharge and dressings from some

13

wounds are sterile after a first dressing, in the large majority smears from both show pyogenic organisms. Dry wounds are likely to be sterile, in the discharges from the moist ones organisms are nearly always found. In spite of this, there is in all these wounds an absence of the clinical signs of inflammation ; there is no redness, heat, pain or swelling, and generally fever is absent. It is our belief that in such wounds the organisms are derived from the surrounding skin and the wound surface, and that the depths are free from infection. This may explain why it is that deep abscesses and cellulitis do not follow this treatment when it can be efficiently carried out.

The Bacteriology and Pathology of wounds are such difficult problems that much time and labour will yet require to be spent on them before entire reliance can be placed upon either or both as the only guides to treatment. Meantime, not having any useful knowledge, I intend to say nothing further as to this,* but to offer some clinical observations which can be repeated easily and which appear to me to be helpful.

Clinical Experiments

The absence of the ordinary signs of inflammation, mentioned above, is one of the most striking features of this method of treatment. When a dressing has been left on an open wound for days or weeks, a slimy, purulent mess may be discovered in it and soaking the wound. On removing this the underlying skin will be found soft, supple and unsodden ; the granulations exceptionally *vascular and active :* and there will be an entire absence of pain.

In order to test the effect of this treatment upon the vitality of the soft tissues, we used it for skin grafting. *The grafts lived.* We have made use of this knowledge, though not

* Two papers by Drs. Louisa Garrett Anderson, Helen Chambers and J. N. Goldsmith deal fully with Clinical, Bacteriological and Chemical effects of this treatment, *Lancet,* March 3rd, 1917.

recommending it as the best method of dealing with skin grafts.

As a test of surgical cleanliness we used catgut sutures, knowing that they offered striking evidence of infection in any wound. In ordinary surgically clean wounds a skin suture of catgut, chromicised or plain, will cause no redness or irritation when properly applied, *i.e.*, only tightly enough to bring about apposition of the wound edges. A mild infection causes a red circle on the skin round the suture, a worse infection makes the red area weep, and a gross infection leads to destruction of the tissues round the suture with pus formation, the suture being cast off as a slough.

In the first case, *i.e.*, when the wound is surgically clean, the buried portion of the suture will be absorbed in a certain number of days according to its size and method of preparation, and this is surely the result of phagocytic action. Our experiments proved that after Bipping infected wounds and using catgut sutures the catgut generally caused no irritation in the skin, and that the buried portion was absorbed at least as quickly as in normal conditions. We also found that catgut sutures smeared with Bipp were absorbed. Our conclusion was that in these wounds infective organisms were either inhibited or destroyed and that phagocytosis was not seriously interfered with by Bipp.

Other observations concerned the effects of this treatment on osteogenesis. After applying it to fractures, it was found that union with the production of considerable callus occurred with exceptional rapidity, and we had the opportunity of watching with X-ray pictures the behaviour of an old cavity in the os calcis filled with Bipp. From an opening through which the Bipp was extruded an exostosis, which required surgical removal, developed of the shape and size of the extruded Bipp. The conclusion drawn was that osteogenesis had been stimulated by the treatment. We are now testing the

17   c

practical value of these observations in bone plating and bone grafting.

Fractures

In the earlier days of the War, next to the knee joint, fractures of the long bones were the most painful and serious lesions requiring treatment. Such frequent dressings as were necessary from profuse suppuration, and the pain of moving the limb, stimulated the development of an output of skilfully devised splints intended to overcome these difficulties. None of these were wholly satisfactory. The most striking advantages of my method of treatment have been observed in this class of case, because, except for the necessary operation, these fractures are now no more trouble than are simple ones. But it is also unfortunately true that the results in War, as in civil cases, are not so good now as they were thirty years ago, when surgeons were less interested in the abdomen and more in the limbs. In treating all

18

fractures, whether military or civil, these rules should be used as a guide :—

1. Render first aid.

2. Examine for complications—local and general.

3. Reduce the fracture.

4. Keep it reduced.

5. Restore function.

Röntgen-ray examinations and pictures have made the treatment of fractures a terror to the majority of doctors, as it is now impossible for those who recognise their responsibility to work without so valuable a guide. Even though responsibility for complete treatment is not accepted, first aid may prevent serious happenings, and vascular and nervous lesions complicating the fracture will not be overlooked if these rules are remembered and applied.

The most important of all teaching relating to the temporary treatment of fractures should be to bear in mind the danger of too tight a bandage. If a patient complains that his bandage is too tight *it must be loosened at once*.

From the variety of splints arriving, it is obvious in any military hospital here how much importance is attached to their use. It is sometimes forgotten that, with very rare exceptions, the most a splint can do is to hold in position a fracture which has already been reduced.

Another principle, taught by Sir Arbuthnot Lane so long ago that it should have now obtained universal recognition, is that any fracture with much displacement can but rarely be reduced by manipulation. If anyone doubts this, the *X*-ray will soon make it clear to him. These two principles are important aids in the consideration of the treatment of fractures. They suggest, first, that very simple splints serve for the majority of cases, and, secondly, that operations will be more frequently performed in fracture cases in the future than they have been in the past.

The ingenious and simple splints of Sir

Robert Jones are so well known as to require no special recommendation, for they are in almost universal use and for transport purposes are unequalled. My own preference is for Gooch splinting, because I know that if I cannot succeed with this it will be difficult for me to get a good result at all. Continuous extension, with weight and pulley and plaster of paris, are often useful additions to the Gooch splints.

Operations for Fracture

During the first year of the War experience of the operative treatment of fractures was so calamitous that an order was sent round from Headquarters to surgical hospitals to the effect that no more fracture operations were to be done. In civil practice surgeons had already learned the danger of operating on compound fractures, but they had not so fully appreciated that properly to repair a simple fracture by operation required exceptional skill, a rigorous technique and a trained hospital team. Given these conditions, compound fractures may be safely and successfully plated if my method of wound treatment be employed, and finding they do well we are using plates for an increasing number of cases.

Necrosis

Following union of septic fractures, a sinus may persist and this almost invariably leads to a portion of dead bone, which may be felt with a probe and shows in an X-ray plate as a sequestrum. Necrosis is one of the end results of bone infection. A separated portion of bone will live and take its part in repair if inflammation of it can be prevented, but if serious infection occurs the resulting destruction is certain to cause the death of completely detached portions, and the consequent circulatory stasis is likely to determine the death of pieces which have not lost their ordinary vascular supply, and are still adherent. Necrosis, the result of sepsis,

22

has been the chief cause of the worst deformities following union of fractures, particularly of the femur. This is because if healing of the wound could be obtained it appeared to be cheap at any price, and the fracture was apt to be neglected. Hundreds of men, a burden to themselves and a serious loss to the nation, are now incapacitated owing to bone sepsis, so that the treatment of infected fractures is of the greatest importance. Our experience has taught us that the great majority do extraordinarily well when treatment can be undertaken within the first week after the injury. This suggests that serious infection takes an unusually long time to develop and spread in fractured bones. Later, if the septic area can be exposed and treated, arrest of any further infection may be safely anticipated, and in the worst cases, although necrosis has already occurred, amelioration of the conditions can be so far brought about as to allow of dressings being left on for some days.

BIPP TREATMENT OF WAR WOUNDS

Treatment of Fractures

In early cases we have treated the wounds in the same way as those of the soft parts, viz., by free exposure of the depths of the wound and of the fractured bone; removal of all dirt, foreign bodies and entirely loose portions of bone; dry gauze, then spirit gauze mopping; rubbing Bipp into all parts of the wound, including the fractured portions of bone; and suture of the wound with sterile Bipped sutures of thick silk. Suitable dressings and splints have then been applied and left undist rbed for from two to six weeks, when the fracture has usually been found to be united, and if there has not been too much destruction of the skin to prevent apposition of the wound edges, this should be healed.

Treatment of Necrosis

Before we learned how to deal with these cases they were unsatisfactory and serious.

A " septic flare-up " often followed removal of the sequestra by operation, more bone necrosis followed and repeated operations too frequently failed to bring about recovery. X-ray pictures, taken beforehand, are a valuable aid during the operation, but, in addition, a long probe introduced into the sinus should be kept in contact with the dead bone until the cavity in which it is lying is exposed. After the usual skin cleansing, scar tissue surrounding the sinus and the sinus itself should be excised, and a free incision made down to the probe through the periosteum. By separating the periosteum round the probe, an opening into the bone-cavity is revealed. The bony roof of the cavity should then be chipped away with a gouge, till its interior and contained sequestra are fully exposed and the loose bone is removed. Granulations should be scooped out of the cavity by a sharp spoon, followed by rubbing with dossils of dry gauze. It is of the greatest importance at this stage to see the whole of the bone-cavity. For this purpose, we have a search-light and reflector ready, if needed for full exploration, because lack of this is a frequent cause of failure after necrosis operations. The wound, after being cleaned with dry gauze, then spirit gauze and Bipped, should be closed by sutures, which may necessitate further separation of the skin from the surrounding tissues, or the formation of a flap, which may be the most satisfactory covering.

Sinus

A sinus is best described as a tubular ulcer with something at the bottom preventing it from healing—but after operation for necrosis this something may be impossible to find. Occasionally one of these persistent sinuses, which appears to lead to nothing definite, can be cured by a few injections of Beck's paste, carefully made. If after three or four injections there is no response it

26

should be opened up and dressed from the bottom.

Chronic Bone-cavities

A persistent sinus after satisfactory necrosis operations is commonly due to an unhealed cavity in the bone. The interior of these chronic cavities is lined by tough, fibrous granulations, and outside these a layer of sclerosed bone. They cannot heal because of the rigidity of their walls. Small ones will heal after some such treatment as chipping away the walls to make an open trough and filling this with Bipp, but the larger require to be stimulated and filled by some sort of graft. We have used three varieties of graft (1) muscle with pedicle ; (2) fat with pedicle ; (3) free fat.

Muscle-flaps often require difficult dissection for their transplantation, and more or less mutilation follows their use. Fat pedicled grafts in certain positions are entirely satis-

27

factory. The abundant gluteal fat may be used in this way to fill cavities in the sacrum, ilium or great trochanter ; or that covering the deltoid for those in the upper end of the humerus.

No free graft will live in a septic cavity, or in the presence of irritating antiseptics. After proving that skin grafts could survive treatment by our method, we adopted free fat grafts as best and most easily obtainable, and have now had so many successful cases that we feel justified in saying that recovery should be the rule, and an explanation of failure should be carefully sought for.

After cleansing the surrounding skin, scar tissue and granulations are dissected out or scraped away with a sharp spoon. The cavity is then thoroughly exposed to view by chipping away the roof, its granulation lining is removed with a sharp spoon and the bone is scraped till a vascular surface has been reached. The cavity is now cleansed with dry gauze, followed by spirit gauze, and once more fully explored, if necessary with a search-light. Bipp is packed into it and thoroughly rubbed into the walls, any excess being removed. The bone-cavity is next packed with dry gauze and a dissection made to allow of covering over the cavity without any tension on the skin edges of the wound. The gauze is removed and the cavity filled with fat and the wound sutured. If there is any tension on the wound edges, when the sutures are removed fat appears at the bottom and healing is much delayed, though the grafts have never in our experience been extruded. It is better, if there is any doubt, to cover the grafts with a flap (Figs. 1, 2, and 3.). Either a large enough single fat graft or multiple small pieces, which we prefer, can be used. After months of daily dressing and discharging these cases may be expected to heal in a few weeks. It is interesting to watch in *X*-ray pictures replacement of the fat by bone.

BIPP TREATMENT OF WAR WOUNDS

FIG. I

A large gunshot hole in the upper end of the tibia surrounded by granulations and scar tissue. The scar and granulation tissue were excised by dissection and the bone-cavity was firmly curetted by a sharp spoon until it showed vascular bone. The cavity and wound were then Bipped.

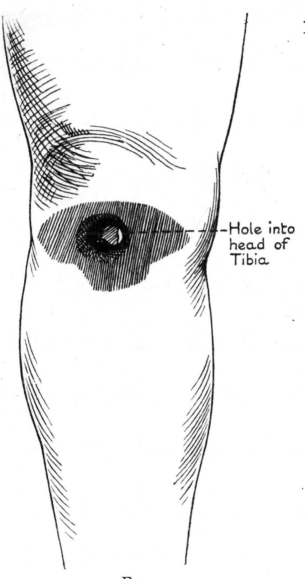

—Hole into
head of
Tibia

FIG. I

31

FIG. 2

A flap with broad pedicle was taken from the upper part of the leg, the wound and flap were again Bipped, and the cavity in the bone was filled up by four portions of fat about $\frac{3}{4}$-inch square, removed from the upper part of the thigh. The flap was sutured in position and scored.

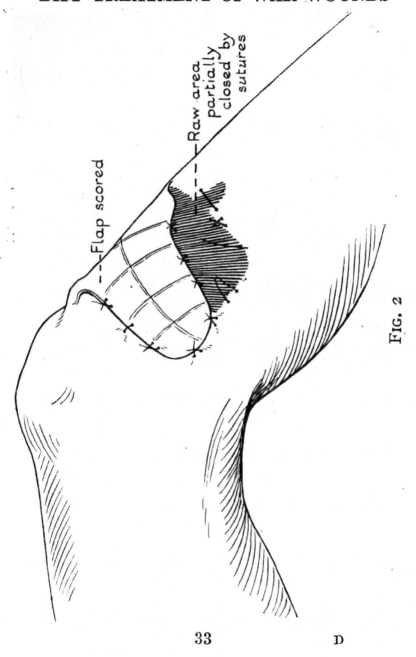

Raw area partially closed by sutures

Flap scored

Fig. 2

FIG. 3

A fortnight later the wound was dressed
for the first time, when the flap was found to
have united by first intention and the raw
surface was covered by healthy granulations. These were skin grafted. Wound
entirely healed in six weeks.

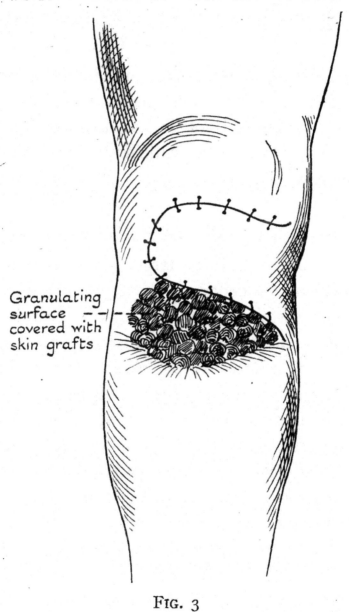

Granulating
surface
covered with
skin grafts

FIG. 3

BIPP TREATMENT OF WAR WOUNDS

Bone Grafts

We are now treating some hopeless-looking cases in which bone has been entirely lost by the use of bone grafts and Bipp, but have not yet advanced sufficiently to make any report (Fig. 4).

Wounded Joints

War wounds of large joints were always serious, exceptionally painful, and ended with certainty in anchylosis till recently. At the present time (December, 1917) there are in my wards seven cases of complicated wounds of the knee-joint Bipped in France. All of them arrived without pain or constitutional disturbance, and in each there is already fair movement of the joint. This is in striking contrast to the condition of cases arriving only one year ago.

The treatment of wounded joints differs from that of other regions. The joint, after cleaning the skin with 1–20 carbolic lotion, should be freely opened and its purulent contents, as far as possible, evacuated by gentle squeezing. Then a quantity of Bipp (about a teaspoonful) is ladled into the joint, the opening is closed by interrupted sutures and the medicament is distributed by gentle massage of the closed joint. Washing or scrubbing or any avoidable manipulation of the synovial membrane should be avoided. Extension is applied by an apparatus which will ensure that it is continuous, and splints are so used as to secure complete rest. In cases where irretrievable damage has not been inflicted on the bones and joints, it is possible to secure restoration of function in the joint, so that no fixation apparatus should be worn after the wound is healed.

For a wound of the knee-joint the same treatment may suffice, but if it is complicated by fracture or retained missile or has resisted the milder measures suggested, the operation as published by me in the *British Medical Journal* of October 20th, 1917, should be

BIPP TREATMENT OF WAR WOUNDS

Fig. 4

A portion of radius lost through a healed gunshot wound replaced by a graft of the whole thickness of the fibula, including the periosteum. The radius was too soft to hold a plate and screws, so the graft was attached to it by catgut ligatures. The graft shows drill-holes to allow of the entrance of new blood-vessels. Excision of the scar left a large skin gap which could not be brought together. The bone graft was buried by suture of the flexor muscles over it with catgut. The raw surface was dressed with gauze covered by a thin layer of Bipp. Dressing unchanged for six weeks.

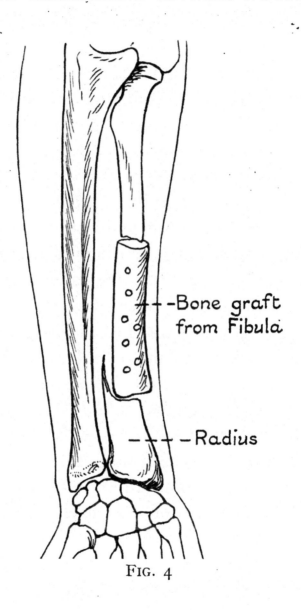

FIG. 4

performed without delay. It is done in the following steps :—

1. Apply an ankle gaiter or extension strapping or glue dressing below the knee.

2. Disinfect the skin surrounding the wound and the joint (1–20 carbolic).

3. Apply a tourniquet.

4. Cover up everything except the knee with sterile and moist antiseptic towels.

5. Open the joint through a horseshoe-shaped incision, dividing the patellar ligament and the musculo-aponeurotic structures on each side of the joint, but avoiding damage to the lateral ligaments on either.

6. Reflect the patella, exposing the joint and subcrural pouch. *Mop*—gently, very gently, not *scrub or wipe*—with dry sterile gauze, any discharge from both.

7. Flex the joint fully, and clean the posterior portion of the cavity by *gentle* dry mopping.

8. Gradually extend the joint ; fill it with spirit and gently mop dry.

40

9. Remove the tourniquet with the limb elevated to a right angle and keep it there with the joint compressed under gauze pads for four minutes. Then clamp any bleeding points with Lane's hæmostatic forceps.

10. Rub a thin layer of Bipp over the whole joint surfaces with a finger. Rubber gloves are understood.

11. As soon as bleeding has ceased suture the patellar ligament with strong mattress sutures and close the remainder of the deep incision with interrupted catgut sutures, holding the joint capsule with interrupted sutures of fine catgut. Close the skin with interrupted sutures of thick, dry, sterile silk smeared with Bipp.

12. Dress the wound with gauze wrung out of spirit, and over this abundant cotton-wool, but no bandage.

13. Fix the limb with two—inner and outer—Gooch splints, the inner reaching from perineum to sole of foot, the outer from tip of trochanter to sole. On top of the

ordinary bandage apply an oblique one at the top, another above and below the knee, and one above the ankle, of plaster of paris.

14. As soon as the patient is in bed apply 15 to 25 lb. weight for continuous extension.

Unless there is need the dressing should not be changed for three weeks. As soon after as the wound is healed massage and movements should commence.

Since this paper was published four cases have been operated upon by two of my colleagues in the Northumberland War Hospital, who followed the technique described with efficient thoroughness. Three of these patients have made brilliant recoveries, the fourth was a failure, not from the joint sepsis, which had been arrested, but from a complicating comminuted fracture of the upper end of the tibia, which was not Bipped. This patient recovered after amputation of the thigh.

BIPP TREATMENT OF WAR WOUNDS

Wounds of the Soft Parts

After thorough cleansing by the usual technique, ordinary wounds can be closed by sutures and left undisturbed for three weeks. If it be possible to bring the skin edges into apposition without undue tension, they should then be healed. For sutures we prefer thick silk, dry, sterilised and rubbed with Bipp, and to prevent the sutures from cutting indiarubber drainage tubing is useful. Silk degenerates if dry sterilised more than twice, after this spare quantities should be kept in spirit and dried as required. For the extremities, splints to secure rest are always desirable, and firm compression over abundant cotton-wool by well applied bandages is as important in war as in civil surgery. When much skin has been destroyed the wounds may be lessened in size and healing aided by drawing the edges as nearly together as possible by relaxation incisions and sutures. Tension on the skin and the chance of slough-

43

ing from this and the consequent œdema are materially diminished by scoring the tense skin round the wound (Fig. 5). Much may now be done to cover still larger gaps by transplantation of flaps (Figs. 6 and 7), and the chances of the survival and union of these are multiplied by skin scoring. These wounds should be twice Bipped—first before dissection of the flaps is begun and again when the raw surfaces of the flaps are ready to be fixed into position by sutures.

Cerebral Hernia

The treatment of cerebral hernia used to be a long and trying ordeal to patient, surgeon and nurses. The protruding, fungating and septic brain discharged so freely as to require frequent dressing, and weeks generally passed before diminution of its size gave any hope of its disappearance. In the *British Journal of Surgery*, April, 1917, I published a series of cases in which the hernia had disappeared

44

in from twelve to twenty-four days, under a dressing left unchanged for a week, and that is the rule. The surrounding hair should be removed and the skin cleaned in the ordinary way with 1–20 carbolic lotion. The hernia is then swabbed with spirit and covered up by gauze spread with Bipp, and outside of this cotton-wool and a night-cap bandage. Three of our cases have had a tragic ending, and in all these the onset, symptoms and post-mortem examination were so alike that we now recognise a type. Each of these patients appeared to be well and in good condition for weeks after the head injury, except that a sinus discharging very little was still present. Suddenly severe head-ache with fever developed, and this was followed by signs of cerebro-spinal meningitis terminating in death within a week. Post-mortem examination of all three showed a cerebral abscess containing particles of bone. From the abscess a track led into the lateral ventricle, and diffusion of the in-

·FIG. 5

The wound edges are drawn forward by
sutures attaching the skin to the deep fascia.
The straight relaxation incision is shown on
the opposite side of the scored skin.

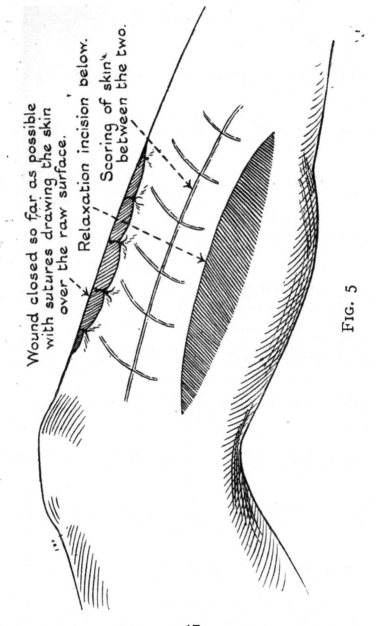

Wound closed so far as possible with sutures drawing the skin over the raw surface.

Relaxation incision below.

Scoring of skin between the two.

Fig. 5

47

FIG. 6

Large shell wound of scalp and fracture
of skull followed by necrosis. The portion
of dead bone removed was loose, surrounded
by pus and lying on a bed of granulations
springing from the dura mater.

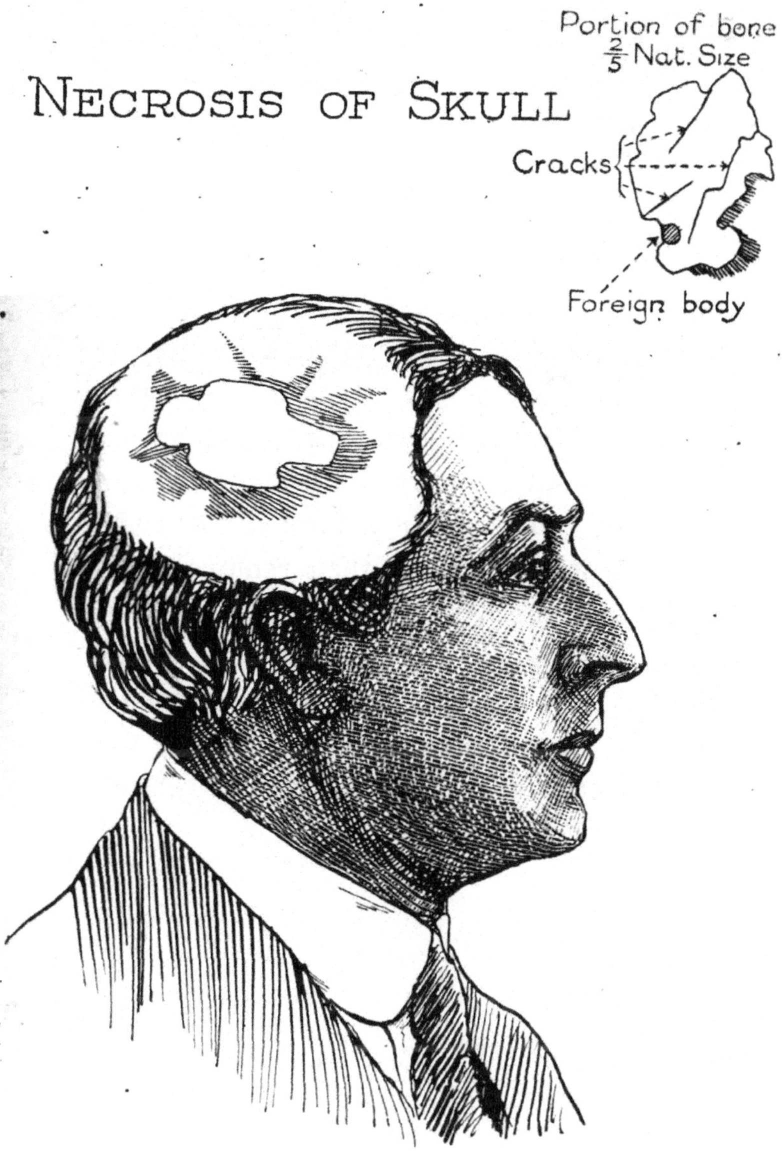

NECROSIS OF SKULL

Portion of bone
$\frac{2}{5}$ Nat. Size

Cracks {

Foreign body

FIG. 6

49   E

FIG. 7

The granulations were scrubbed with dry
gauze, then spirit gauze followed by Bipp.
Flaps considerably scarred were separated
from above and anteriorly, and below and
posteriorly. The under-surfaces of these and
the raw surfaces left by their removal were
Bipped and the flaps sutured over the skull
gap with silkworm gut sutures. The dressings were not changed for a fortnight, when
the flaps were found to be united and the
sutures were removed. Complete healing
in eight weeks.

PLASTIC OPERATION

Raw surface   Raw surface

FIG. 7

51   E 2

fection from this had caused general septic cerebro-spinal meningitis.

Suppuration

Perhaps the most interesting achievement of this method of treatment is its effect on staphylococcic abscesses and the suppuration consequent on streptococcus infections of the lymphatics and cellular tissue.

In treating an abscess our plan is first to clean the skin with 1–20 carbolic lotion, then to open the abscess sufficiently freely to allow of inspection of the whole cavity, aided by a search-light if needful. The cavity is cleaned first by thorough mopping with dry gauze, then it is flushed with spirit and mopped by gauze wet with the same, finally after further inspection its walls are smeared with a thin layer of Bipp, removing all unattached excess. The wound is closed by interrupted thick silk sutures smeared with Bipp, and dressed with sterile gauze, cotton-wool, a firm bandage, and in the case of an extremity a splint to secure rest. The dressing is not changed for from two to three weeks, when we find that healing has often occurred throughout by what looks like first intention.*

In diffuse suppurating lymphangitis and cellulitis some extraordinary results have followed opening and dealing with pus collections in the same manner as for ordinary localised abscess. It has been not rare to find pain, swelling and fever disappear, the red lymphatic vessels become pale, the tenderness and enlargement of the lymphatic glands rapidly melting away and what was a threatening position reduced to one of small importance. It is cases of this sort that lead us to believe that the effects of Bipp spread beyond the site of its implantation, and additional evidence in favour of this view is

---

* " First intention " is an old clinical term, the meaning of which is plain. It is not so well known that histologically every wound heals by the formation of granulation tissue, *i.e.,* cellular proliferation and the formation of new blood-vessels.

the fact that iodide of potassium is constantly found in the urine of patients treated with it. At first, fearing that the withdrawal of potassium salts from the blood *might* be mischievous, we gave our patients daily doses of potass. bicarb., but as it turned out that omission of the medicine was followed by no bad effects, we gradually dropped it.

I have now treated many compound fractures associated with abscess and cellulitis by this method with a success which never ceases to surprise me.

Amputations

The importance of saving as great a length of limb as possible has led us to modify the method of trimming guillotine amputations arriving from France. By making an incision from the granulating surface upwards on that side of the limb most avascular, dissecting the soft parts from the bone or bones hugging them closely, retracting the soft parts with a strong gauze retractor before and during the application of the saw and bringing the granulating surfaces together with sutures over the bone, the stump will be shortened by the smallest possible amount. (Figs. 8 and 9.) In these cases the dressings can be left unchanged for three weeks and sutures should not be taken out before, because if they are removed earlier the flaps are apt to open up in parts. Dressings should be fixed so that they cannot loosen or slip off, and should be voluminous and firmly bandaged to ensure elastic compression of the stump.

Dressings at the Front

It is obvious that my method of treatment should not be used as an emergency one at the Front, and there are several reasons for this.

The first, to which my attention was especially drawn by Surgeon-General Sir George Makins, is the danger of gas gangrene following closure of fresh wounds.

The second is that the technique must be

BIPP TREATMENT OF WAR WOUNDS

Fig. 8

The ordinary guillotine stump as it comes from France. These cases were difficult to handle in 1915, and whatever was done the result usually was sepsis, profuse suppuration and much shortening of the stump. At the present time we seldom remove more than bone. The granulating surface is covered up by gauze wrung out of 1–20 carbolic lotion and the surrounding skin cleansed with the same lotion. The granulating area is then scrubbed with dry gauze, next with gauze wet with spirit and then smeared over with Bipp.

GUILLOTINE STUMP

Skin edge   Bone

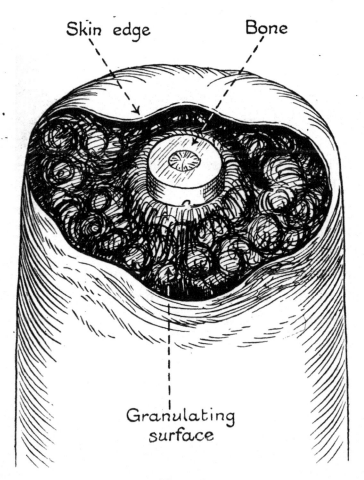

Granulating
surface

FIG. 8

BIPP TREATMENT OF WAR WOUNDS

FIG. 9

It is closed by mattress tension sutures of thick silk and indiarubber tubing, with interrupted sutures of thick silk for the edges of the wound. If there is tension the skin is scored. A voluminous dressing of gauze and sterile wool is *firmly* bandaged on and securely fixed. This is left for three weeks, when the sutures are removed.

REPAIR OF
GUILLOTINE STUMP

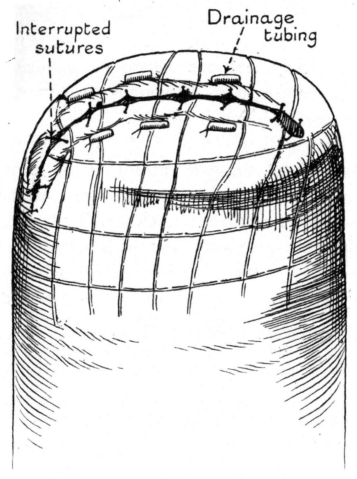

FIG. 9

carried out with such careful attention to detail as to take considerable time.

The third that both bismuth and iodoform may prevent satisfactory X-ray pictures.

Lastly, that it is possible there may be more danger of poisonous absorption of bismuth or iodoform in fresh wounds than in those coming to home hospitals.

For a first dressing A. E. Morison's magnesium sulphate cream is of proved worth.* . . . The wound or wounds should be opened up, cleaned and packed with this cream, dressed with sterile gauze and wool and left for three or four days.

During this time X-ray photographs can

* Method of preparation of the mag. sulph. cream :—
1–5 lb. of magnes. sulph. exsiccatum are mixed with 11 oz. of glycerine carbolic acid (1 in 10). The dried mag. sulph. is in the form of a fine, white powder which contains 12 per cent. less water than ordinary mag. sulph. The glycerine carbolic acid is put in a *hot* mortar and the mag. sulph. added, slowly stirring and mixing with a warm pestle all the time. The result is a thick, white cream, so hydroscopic that if exposed to the air it rapidly absorbs moisture and becomes fluid. To preserve it in a jar is essential.

be made and after the fourth day the danger of gas gangrene developing appears to be small—so that these wounds can then be cleansed and closed by the method I have described.

In all my papers the danger of poisoning from bismuth and iodoform has been noted and the symptoms and signs of it described, especially at length in the *British Journal of Surgery* for April, 1917. Thus : " Our hospital case notes have special reference to this question under the headings—(1) *Temperature :* A rise of temperature, apparently due to absorption, as nothing else could be found to explain it, was noted in some cases, and along with this there was some alteration in (2) *Pulse-rate :* This was quickened. (3) *Emaciation :* In two cases with large multiple wounds freely treated with Bipp there was, in spite of good appetite, progressive emaciation. (4) *Bronzing of the Skin*—This occurred in the above two patients along with (5) *Diarrhœa ;* and (6) *Stomatitis :*

blue patches on the gums and in the mouth (bismuth poisoning) : These were noted in three cases altogether. (7) *Nervous symptoms :* Apathy or delirium was noted in five or six of our cases, and these symptoms have, I learn, been observed by others (iodoform poisoning). (8) *Urine :* Presence of Potassium Iodide. (9) *Excessive discharge from the wound*—A few of our wounds have discharged profusely a slimy, purulent fluid after the application of Bipp, and this we regard as an indication for its removal and replacement by some other form of treatment, as it is especially in these cases that the troubles to which our notes refer have arisen.

" In two of our cases the symptoms have been sufficiently serious to demand cleaning out of the wound, and this is an obvious duty if suspicion of poisoning approaches certainty. In three cases we have noticed dermatitis and pustules develop on the skin surrounding the wound, but this was never a serious drawback—though probably attributable to iodoform " (occasionally to using perchloride of mercury lotion along with it by mistake).

Regarding poisoning, Colonel Gordon Watson, whose statement is based upon thousands of cases, says :—

" There is some danger of poisoning both by bismuth and iodoform, but this danger is reduced to a minimum if the paste is merely lightly rubbed over the wound surface and all excess removed, and the early toxic effects may be rapidly reduced by washing out the wound with peroxide of hydrogen and the administration of alkalis internally.

" When Bipp is used on a large wound surface, symptoms of combined bismuth and iodoform poisoning, such as the blue-black line on the gums, black tongue, red rash, rise of temperature, emaciation, sunken eyes, delirium or mental aberrations, must be watched for.

" It is often difficult to differentiate between the symptoms of wound toxæmia and Bipp toxæmia.

" Toxic effects are not so frequent or so serious as to weigh at all against the advantage of its use, if proper care is exercised."

I now offer the lessons taught by my own experience of the paste. In the early stages of this treatment when we used it freely, filling large wounds with it and having no regard for the quantity retained, some cases of serious absorption occurred. There has been no death attributable to bismuth or iodoform absorption in the Northumberland War Hospital among the several thousand cases treated with it. A single case was reported to me as having died of iodoform poisoning a few days after he had been Bipped. He had been delirious and then comatose before his death. A post-mortem examination showed that he died from septic cerebro-spinal meningitis, and search for the cause revealed a small wound through a spinal lamina into his spinal canal. This communicated with a small septic wound of the back to which no importance had been attached. A small piece of shell was lying on the cord.

For more than a year there has been no evidence of absorption discoverable in our cases, with the exception of an occasional blue line round the necks of some teeth. The patients in which this appeared had large freely discharging wounds, and were usually of fair complexion, delicate and anæmic in appearance, and had dirty teeth. In civil cases I have had opportunities for using Bipp in serious and large fresh wounds. No patient so treated has shown any symptoms of absorption. It therefore seems justifiable to say that dangerous absorption results either from mistakes in technique or from the use of a faulty paste. If any excess of Bipp be removed after rubbing it well into the wound surfaces, and a satisfactory paste be employed, serious trouble is not likely to arise. A satisfactory paste should leave a thin, adherent, even smear over the surface of the wound, but many preparations of it sold do not fulfil this requirement. To overcome this difficulty, Sergeant Hunter, dispenser to the Northumberland War Hospital, has undertaken to supervise the preparation sold by W. Owen and Son, Chemists, Barras Bridge, Newcastle-upon-Tyne, and Mr. Sidney Dunstan, of the Dispensary, Royal Victoria Infirmary, that sent out by the Numol Company, 3, College Street, Newcastle-upon-Tyne.

I entertain no doubt that lives and limbs have been saved by this method which would have been lost by any other known to me. Ward visits, which were previously a painful duty, have now been transformed into an interesting quest. Dr. Pirrie (formerly Dr. Evelyn Ritson), my resident surgeon, and I have 200 beds under our charge, and with few exceptions I do all dressings in an operating theatre myself on one or two mornings of the week. Only small or superficial wounds are dressed by nurses in the wards. Daily dressings for all our cases would have overwhelmed double our present staff of nurses and orderlies, and in addition to this saving the amount economised in dressings is considerable.

INDEX

69

INDEX

INDEX

INDEX